Printed in Great Britain
by Amazon

51042306R00068